DEAR GANDHI:

Now what?

Letters from Ground Zero.

Jim and Shelley Douglass
Illustrated by Bill Livermore

new society publishers

Philadelphia, PA   Santa Cruz, CA

Inquiries regarding requests to reprint all or part of
Dear Gandhi: Now What? Letters from Ground Zero should be addressed to:

New Society Publishers
4527 Springfield Avenue
Philadelphia, PA 19143

ISBN
0-86571-124-0 Hardcover
0-86571-125-9 Paperback

Printed in the United States of America, on partially recycled paper.

Cover and book design by Barbara Hirshkowitz.
Cover and text illustrations by Bill Livermore.

To order directly from the publisher, add $1.50 to the price for the first
copy, 50¢ each additional. Send check or money order to:
New Society Publishers
PO Box 582
Santa Cruz, CA 95061-0582

New Society Publishers is a project of the New Society Educational
Foundation, a nonprofit, tax-exempt, public foundation. Opinions
expressed in this book do not necessarily represent positions of the New
Society Educational Foundation.

Publisher's Note

When I read the paper in the morning, it is always in the same order. First the comics and then the advice columns. After that I figure I am ready to face the rest of what our local paper reports as news.

When we receive our copy of *Ground Zero* I always turn to "Dear Gandhi" first. *Ground Zero* is a lot more interesting to read than the local paper, but "Dear Gandhi" helps keep it all in perspective.

It is important, as we go about our work of building a world we all want to live in, to remember to keep a sense of humor about it all. Gandhi did! "Dear Gandhi" helps me do that. I hope you enjoy it as much as all of us at New Society Publishers do.

In peace,

Ellen Sawislak
for New Society Publishers
May 4, 1987

Introduction

The Ground Zero newspaper originated in a brainstorming session one winter afternoon in 1982. Eight members of the newly formed core community at Ground Zero Center for Nonviolent Action sat around and dreamed of publishing a journal of opinion, a newspaper that would report and reflect upon the seven-year-old campaign in the Pacific Northwest against the Trident submarine and missile system. First we agreed that we'd report news of the campaign and that we'd reflect on nonviolence. Then we added ingredients essential to any newspaper: an advice column and comics. The advice column could only be called "Dear Gandhi"—a nonviolent rival to "Dear Abby."

Gandhi was an obvious choice for us because we have been engaged in a Gandhian experiment in nonviolence during the course of the work here. Gandhi's idea of experimenting in truth, finding what we could of the truth and then acting upon it, was a basic pattern for the Trident campaign. As our experiment developed, we have been struck by the aptness of much of Gandhi's thought, here on the other side of the globe and many years after his own work. A journalist and publisher, Gandhi published up to three newspapers at the same time. His papers often included columns of his advice to readers. Gandhi's insights often spoke to our condition in ways that enlightened. Gandhi had accompanied us through the campaign from 1975 to 1982, and we felt that he was important to our continued work.

When we looked for a graphic artist for our newspaper who could capture our ideas in pictures, Bill Livermore appeared. We found him in San Antonio, Texas, by answering an ad in *Sojourners* magazine, and have been repeatedly thankful for his patience with us and his talent with pen and ink. Although he has never been to Ground Zero, Bill, too, has been an important part of our work. His classic portrait of columnist Gandhi with quill pen in hand, on the cover of this book, has graced every Ground Zero newspaper. Bill's illustrations in these pages capture the spirit of Gandhi and his motley crew of correspondents.

The nonviolent campaign against Trident began with the resignation of Lockheed missile designer Robert Aldridge, who worked on the re-entry vehicle for Trident missiles. Bob's work led him to the knowledge that the United States was building systems capable of a disarming first strike, and his conscience called him to resign. His resignation and the analysis he shared with us inspired the January 1975 formation of Pacific Life Community, a small intentional community committed to resisting the coming of Trident to the Pacific Northwest. Believing that our culture's reliance upon violence is a central root of the arms race and other forms of injustice, Pacific Life Community committed itself to "seek the truth of a nonviolent way of life," both personally and politically. Personally we tried to confront our racism, sexism, consumerism—all the isms that allowed us to violate others. Politically we chose to experiment with nonviolent actions resisting the Trident, a system that seemed to epitomize all the violence of our society. In 1975, the homeport for Trident was under construction at Bangor on the Hood Canal in Washington state. Pacific Life Community began to raise the issue of Trident and first strike through community education and direct action; within three years a broader community of concern had formed, including several groups much larger than Pacific Life Community.

By 1978 and 1979 - the talks, marches, rallies, and civil disobedience actions had in fact raised awareness of the lethal potential of the Trident system. People on both sides of the U.S.-Canadian border were concerned enough to journey to the base itself, three to four thousand strong, and to risk arrest by the hundreds. At the same time, some of us who had originally founded the campaign became aware that our nonviolent actions were experienced by those in the Kitsap County community as a form of violence. We were in fact closing the minds we most wanted to open because our actions were seen as a form of condemnation without any openness to listening. Kitsap County, a rural county on a peninsula fifteen miles from Seattle, has a proud tradition of cooperation with the Navy, and a strong economic dependence upon the military. Most of those who hold jobs in the county are dependent upon the military for paychecks. When we marched down Clear Creek Road to the Trident base, those

3

people felt condemned, and their hostility to us grew.

In response to this concern, nine people came together to form Ground Zero Center for Nonviolent Action. Ground Zero, a piece of land sharing 330 feet of barbed-wire fence with the Trident base, gave us the opportunity to have a continuous nonviolent presence in the county, and to form friendships with those whose work we resisted. We made the downpayment on the Ground Zero property in 1977, committing ourselves to a long-term presence in this Navy-dominated area. We wanted to experiment with Gandhi's idea that the enemy has a piece of the truth, and with the religious teaching of love for the enemy. We recognized that in our minds the Navy had become the enemy. We wanted to learn to walk the fine line between hating the sin and loving the sinner, recognizing that we, too, were complicit in violence and thus also sinners.

Ground Zero has gone through stages of growth and changes in community. The group that met in 1982 was the embryo of the present core community, a small intentional community that carries on the work of the day-to-day Trident campaign on the Kitsap Peninsula. The year that the Ground Zero newspaper was founded, 1982, was a watershed year for us because the first Trident submarine, the USS *Ohio*, arrived then and was deployed from Bangor. Some of "Dear Gandhi's" first questions came from people involved in the Peace Blockade to stop the USS *Ohio*, an effort organized by Ground Zero and other friends which resulted in forty people in fifteen small boats and two fifty-foot sailboats preparing to place themselves in the path of the monster submarine. The blockade attracted a great deal of attention from both the government and the media. Ninety-nine Coast Guard cutters were deployed to stop it. On the day the USS *Ohio* arrived, the Coast Guard hosed both blockaders and blockade supporters out of the small boats. The blockaders were arrested and held at gunpoint. Gandhi had a chuckle out of the huge amount of force that did not succeed in keeping an idea at bay. Trident had indeed arrived in Kitsap County, and one local editor said that the Navy's response to the resistance went a long way toward proving the truth of our argument that Trident is a first strike weapon.

As submarines continued to arrive at Bangor, hundreds of warheads and missile motors were delivered by train to be assembled and deployed. In answer to shipments of missile parts, the Agape Community grew up along the tracks between Salt Lake City, Utah, and Bangor. The community tracked and resisted the movement of weapons trains; later the same community grew to include tracks travelled by the White, or Nuclear, Train from the Pantex Plant in Amarillo, Texas. People along the tracks take responsibility for the arms race through education and action, including sitting on the tracks in front of trains to stop arms shipments. Gandhi has commented on issues raised during the tracks campaign, holding us to our nonviolent commitment and helping us to deal with feelings evoked by the trains.

Organizing efforts have been continuous, and so has the bedrock work of building relationships with Navy people in Kitsap County, discussing ideas of nonviolence, learning a bit more day by day about how to be disarmed people. Weekly leafletting of workers at local bases, begun in September of 1978, continues unbroken for nine years. Workers have resigned their jobs or taken other actions to support the campaign. We have come to confront our own violence more deeply, both on a personal level and at the level of complicity with a violent political and economic system.

Throughout this process the Ground Zero newspaper has been the vehicle of our reflection. We sometimes feel that we would never sit down and think had we not committed ourselves to publishing a quarterly newspaper. "Dear Gandhi" helps to keep us sane. We are impressed, as we write these columns, with the relevance of Gandhi's insights to our own questions and problems. Gandhi understood violence, complicity, and the human heart. The original Gandhi quotes, identified in this book by asterisks, have become precepts for the work we're doing. His wisdom both comforts and challenges us.

"Dear Gandhi" is important to us also as a way of laughing at ourselves and our ridiculous efforts to learn simple things. Friends of ours who knew Gandhi tell us that he had a marvelous sense of humor, laughing often at himself, and with his friends. By creating Gandhian comments on our own situation, we try to share the gentle balloon-bursting side of Gandhi—making fun of our own pretensions, restoring proportion to life. A few critics have taken us to task, arguing that a "Dear Gandhi" column, and especially our zany replies in his name, show disrespect to Gandhi himself. We believe that laughter is a sign of love, and through our work we have come to love that quirky old man. Laughter has helped to keep us sane many times as we looked at the awesome power arrayed against us, and then at the scant resources at our disposal. Laughter, and faith in that Being toward whom Gandhi points us, have helped keep us going through many dark hours. We expect more dark hours before we're done, and we expect Gandhi's gentle spirit to accompany us through them. "Dear Gandhi" is a halting attempt to share some of the humor and wackiness of the work at Ground Zero, to lighten the load for all of us.

We are grateful to New Society Publishers for the opportunity to share these Gandhi letters, and especially to Ellen Sawislak for lightening the load of preparation. Her perseverance in bringing this book to press has shown that she has a good supply of that most revolutionary virtue of all, patience. Thank you, Ellen.

If you'd like to keep up with Gandhi's thoughts and other news from Ground Zero, you can subscribe to our paper (donation, no subscription fee) by writing:

Ground Zero
16159 Clear Creek Road NW
Poulsbo, WA 98370

Jim Douglass   Shelley Douglass

About the Authors

Jim Douglass is an activist, writer and teacher. Author of three books (*The Nonviolent Cross* [MacMillan, 1968], *Resistance and Contemplation* [Doubleday, 1972], and *Lightning East to West* [Crossroads, 1983]), he served as a theological advisor on questions of nuclear war and conscientious objection to Catholic bishops at the Second Vatican Council in Rome (1962–1965). He has taught theology at the University of Hawaii, at Bellarmine College (Louisville, Kentucky), and at the University of Notre Dame.

In 1977, with his wife Shelley, Jim helped found the Ground Zero Center for Nonviolent Action next to the Trident nuclear submarine base outside Seattle, Washington. Since then, the Douglasses have worked to develop an extended nonviolent community across the United States of people watching and vigiling by the tracks of the "White Train," which carries nuclear weapons through some 250 towns and cities. In the course of the past ten years, Jim has spent more than eighteen months in prison for repeated acts of civil disobedience aimed at public education concerning the Trident and the White Train.

Shelley Douglass has been active in nonviolent movements since the early 1960s, with involvement in the Catholic Worker, the Civil Rights movement, the anti-Vietnam War movement, and the feminist movement. She is a candidate for the ministry in the United Church of Canada and currently serves as Chairperson of the National Council of the Fellowship of Reconciliation, a national religious pacifist organization. Shelley's articles on faith, feminism and nonviolence have appeared in *Fellowship, Sojourners, The Catholic Agitator,* and *Ground Zero.*

Shelley lives with her husband Jim and her son Thomas on the edge of the Trident nuclear submarine base in Bangor, Washington. In August, 1983 she completed serving her fifth jail sentence for civil disobedience in response to the threat of Trident.

As a member of the core community of the Ground Zero Center for Nonviolent Action, Shelley is committed to the exploration of nonviolence as a way of life. The work of Ground Zero includes reaching out to Navy and civilian personnel in this highly militarized area, education, planning and training in nonviolence, and organizing of the national campaign along the tracks taken by trains carrying nuclear weapons for Trident to Bangor, WA.

Dear Gandhi,

What if you were alone with your grandmother and she were viciously attacked by a heavyweight boxer armed with brass knuckles? Would you remain nonviolent?

Sincerely,
Earnest Truth Seeker

Dear Earnest,

Following Grandmother's warning, I would pull her shag rug out from under the attacker's feet as he crosses the threshold. That would cause him to fall so that his chin would come to rest comfortably on the far side of the little pillow on which Grandmother rests her feet. The brass knuckles would fly through the air and land harmlessly in the kitchen sink. Grandmother and I would then offer our chagrined visitor tea.

If that doesn't work, Grandmother has other ideas.

Nonviolence demands creativity.

Gandhi

Dear Gandhi,

When we are arrested for trying to stop the USS *Ohio* this summer, people are going to accuse us of being selfish and obstructive. How can we explain our position?

Sincerely,
Ms. Understood

Dear Ms. U,

We can say simply this: We will not submit to this great wrong, not merely because it will destroy us, but because it is destroying you as well.

Gandhi*

Gandhi*   *indicates a quotation from Gandhi's work*

Dear Gandhi,

Many people, including our Archbishop, are advocating noncooperation with taxes in resistance to nuclear arms. Doesn't this tactic create unnecessary suffering? Wouldn't it be better to wait until we have persuaded everyone to agree with us before we act?

Sincerely,
Bea Sure

Dear Bea,

Every citizen is responsible for every act of her or his government. And it is quite proper to support it so long as the actions of the government are bearable. But when they hurt a person and his or her nation, it becomes this person's duty to withdraw their support.

If a father does injustice, it is the duty of his children to leave the parental roof. If a government does a grave injustice the subject must withdraw cooperation wholly or partially, sufficiently to wean the ruler from wickedness.

In each case there is an element of suffering whether mental or physical. Without such suffering it is not possible to attain freedom.

Gandhi*

Dear Gandhi,

Thanks to reading *Ground Zero*, I am now aware of the Nuclear Train and the missile motors trains, and I want to stop them from running any more by organizing a general strike of railway workers. But I don't know anything about trains, don't know any railway workers, and don't know how to organize a strike. Is there a nonviolent technique you can recommend for success in organizing a national railway strike?

Sincerely,
Railroad Ignoramus Pacifus

Dear R.I.P.,

Try trains-national paralysis.

Gandhi

Dear Gandhi,

Here is a question which you may find easy to handle but which many people—even in the peace movement—struggle with: Isn't it too late to turn around the wheels of history and prevent a nuclear war?

Ingrid Rogers
Manchester College

Dear Ingrid,

To say it is impossible because it is difficult, is not in consonance with the spirit of the age. Things undreamt of are daily being seen, the impossible is ever becoming possible. We are constantly being astonished these days at the amazing discoveries in the field of violence. But I maintain that far more undreamt of and seemingly impossible discoveries will be made in the field of nonviolence.

*Gandhi**

12

Dear Gandhi,

What about the Russians?

Sincerely,
The Pentagon

Dear Pentagon,

Tolstoy is my friend. I don't know the others very well but I suggest that you especially make a point of meeting them. It could make a world of difference.

Gandhi

Dear Gandhi,

I am getting tired of protesting and resisting all the evil-doers in the world. It seems to me that it would be much quicker and more effective to remove a few of the worst evils and start all over. We do not have much time to waste in converting our opponents when people are starving and the world may blow up. Why should I try to remain nonviolent?

Sincerely,
Peace Now

Dear Now,

However much I may sympathize with and admire worthy motives, I am an uncompromising opponent of violent methods even to serve the noblest of causes. Experience convinces me that permanent good can never be the outcome of untruth and violence. I feel that progress toward the goal will be in exact proportion to the purity of our means. This method may appear to be long, perhaps too long, but I am convinced that it is the shortest.

Gandhi*

Dear Gandhi,

In reading this issue of *Ground Zero*, I keep coming across reports of people praying by the tracks of the Nuclear Train—or appeals to *Ground Zero*'s readers to meet the Nuclear Train with faith and prayer.

I do not believe in God, Gandhi, and I don't pray. But I do revere life. I identify my life with all that lives, and want to sustain life on earth through nonviolent action. Is that good enough?

Sincerely,
Puzzled by Prayer

Dear Puzzled,

Truth, as you know and love it most deeply, is God. God as truth and love abides in the human heart and in all that lives. If you revere life and identify your life with other lives, including those on the Nuclear Train, you will have realized the truth of God more deeply than by any conscious prayer.

Gandhi*

Dear Gandhi,

I make my living as a baritone singing "The Star Spangled Banner" before professional football games.

Recently I noticed that some of the words of our national anthem don't correspond to my commitment to nonviolence. For reasons of conscience I have therefore been considering changing those words in the course of my next pre-game rendition to something more peaceful.

Do you have any suggestions?

Sincerely,
Voice of Conscience

Dear Voice,

I suggest that you wear a helmet and shoulder pads.

Gandhi

Dear Gandhi,

What do you understand by "civil disobedience"?

Sincerely,
Ready to Act(?)

Dear Ready(?),

Disobedience to be civil must be sincere, respectful, restrained, never defiant, must be based upon some well-understood principle, must not be capricious and above all, must have no ill will or hatred behind it.

Gandhi*

Dear Gandhi,

I believe deeply in your teachings on nonviolence. I have been trying to convince people of the value and necessity of living this way, especially on the national level, but all I get is arguments as to how it won't work. How can I answer their objection?

Sincerely,
A Frustrated Teacher

Dear Frustrated,

Those who believe in the simple truths I have laid down can propagate them only by living them. Your object should be to convert, not to coerce. Avoid artificiality in all things—act naturally and only from inward conviction.

Gandhi*

Dear Gandhi,

As a chaplain in the U.S. Navy, I would like your advice on how to preach on Jesus' teaching, "Love your enemies," to the crew members of a Trident submarine.

Sincerely,
Preacher at Sea

Dear Preacher at Sea,

Give each of them a conscientious objector discharge application; then fill one out yourself.

Gandhi

Dear Gandhi,

I have just received a letter from my insurance company suggesting that I take out a $5 million liability insurance policy. Their letter says that I can be sued for that much if someone is injured "using your recreational vehicle or golf cart...or even if your landscaper fell on your front steps."

This creates a moral dilemma for me: I already have so much insurance that I'm borrowing from loan companies to pay for all the policies. But in order to be responsible to my loved ones, shouldn't I take out this policy, too? What if my landscaper does fall down and sue me, and what if I should happen to die shortly thereafter, leaving my family to deal with his $5 million suit?

Sincerely,
Safe Provider

Dear Safe,

Give your recreation vehicle and golf cart to your landscaper as soon as possible. You might also want to accompany him down your front steps on the way to the garage to pick them up.

Gandhi

Dear Gandhi,

I don't see how I can continue to support my government's nuclear weapons policy, but I question what will happen to me and to my family if I do not cooperate. I don't see any value in taking on suffering when it is avoidable. What do you think?

Sincerely,
Cautious

Dear Cautious,

We must voluntarily put up with the losses and inconveniences that arise from having to withdraw our support from a government that is ruling against our will. We must refuse to wait for the wrong to be righted till the wrong-doer has been roused to a sense of his iniquity. We must not, for fear of ourselves or others having to suffer, remain participants in it. But we must combat the wrong by ceasing to assist the wrong-doer directly or indirectly. In each case there will be an element of suffering whether mental or physical. Without such suffering it is not possible to attain freedom.

Gandhi*

Dear Gandhi,

I find myself living in an affluent country and among affluent people. I know that some people are hungry in this country, and more are hungry abroad. But the President's Commission on Hunger says this is not a serious problem, so why should I worry? Why is there all this fuss about a few hungry people?

Sincerely,
Well-Fed and Annoyed

Dear Annoyed,

I suggest that we are thieves in a way. If I take anything that I do not need for my own immediate use and keep it, I steal it from somebody else. I venture to suggest that it is the fundamental law of Nature, without exception, that she produces enough for our wants from day to day, and if everybody took enough for oneself and nothing more, there would be no pauperism, no one dying of starvation in this world. But so long as we have this inequality, so long are we stealing. If somebody else possesses more than I do, so be it. But I do say that those of us who want to see light out of darkness have to follow this rule in our own lives: We do not dare possess anything more than we actually need.

Gandhi*

Dear Gandhi,

I am a nonviolent activist. I am also angry. I hate the people who do all the terrible things I see. I believe that hatred is justified. What do you say?

Sincerely,
Furious

Dear Furious,

We dare not rest content so long as the poison of hatred is allowed to permeate society. This struggle is a stupendous effort at conversion. We aimed at nothing less than the conversion of the English. You must convert those you feel are your opponents. It can never be done by harboring ill-will and still pretending to follow nonviolence. Let those therefore who want to follow the path of nonviolence and yet harbor ill-will retrace their steps and repent of the wrong they have done to themselves and the world.

Gandhi*

Dear Gandhi,

What would you do if you were made dictator for a day?

Sincerely,
Wishing You Were King

Dear Wishing,

I would not accept it in the first place, but if it did happen I would spend it cleaning the stables of the Viceroy's house. It is disgraceful that under the very nose of the Viceroy such poverty and squalor should exist.

Gandhi

Dear Gandhi,

A friend asked me what I thought about trying to sit in front of the White Train. I told him I thought it was a good idea, but that I wouldn't go onto the tracks myself unless I was relatively free of hope or expectation that I would be removed by anyone or anything but the train, and that I didn't have that much "toosh." What do you think?

Sincerely,
Not Enough Toosh

Dear Toosh,

I agree that civil disobedience requires a spirit of giving one's life, but that spirit should be present in all our works. It is a spirit that comes from a life of constructive work and meditation. Your task is to open yourself to that spirit. Then you will live naturally in such a way as to develop it. That is the only track you need be concerned about being on.

Gandhi

Dear Gandhi,

Why did you wear a loincloth to negotiate with the highest representative of the British Empire?

Sincerely,
Deb O. Nair

Dear Deb,

To save them further embarrassment.

Gandhi

Dear Gandhi,

What is true self-defense?

Sincerely,
Believer in Being Prepared

Dear Believer,

True defense lies along the path of non-retaliation. Someone might say, "If through such nonviolent resistance the defender is likely to lose his or her own life, how can it be called self-defense? Jesus lost his life on the cross and Pilate won."

I do not agree. Jesus has won as the world's history has abundantly shown. What does it matter if the body was dissolved in the process, so long as by Christ's act of non-resistance the forces of good were released in society?

Gandhi*

Dear Gandhi,

Sometimes I come to leaflet on Thursday mornings, and I am impressed by the friendliness of most of the workers at Puget Sound Naval Shipyard. But there are a few people who glare or call me names or even spit at me. What can I do in response to those people?

Sincerely,
Scared

Dear Scared,

You can love them. It is not nonviolent if we merely love those that love us. It is nonviolent only when we love those that hate us. I know how difficult it is to follow this grand Law of Love. But are not all great and good things difficult to do? Love of the hater is most difficult of all. But by the grace of God even this most difficult thing becomes easy to accomplish if we want to do it.

Gandhi*

24

Dear Gandhi,

How can we stop Trident?

Sincerely,
Ev Ray Body

Dear Ev Ray Body,

Read Ground Zero, *even if it is a bit pretentious, and your local paper, and act on both.*

Join the Vigil of Hope, the Agape Community, and the Peace Blockade. If you're in the Navy, don't re-enlist.

Believe that people operating Trident are good people. Likewise the people resisting it. We all need to change.

Get down your Bible and read about Jesus as if he had something entirely new to say to you. Pray harder than you ever have before that you discover what that is. Ditto with Buddha or the peaceful prophet of your choice.

Pray some more, and join me on the Hood Canal.

Here's hoping,
Gandhi

Dear Gandhi,

The last issue of *Ground Zero* ran a series of articles about people resigning Trident-related jobs, reducing lifestyles, resisting war taxes. Almost all these people were married with children. Sometimes *Ground Zero* looks like a family album.

Isn't this pretty un-American? Are these people saying that the bigger your family the more willing you should be to give up your job or go to jail for peace?

Sincerely,
Insurance Agent Questioning My Existence

Dear Insurance Agent,

Yes, parents should be prepared to resign jobs and go to jail for the sake of peace in the human family. God will provide for them and their children. As Jesus says in the Sermon on the Mount, "Seek first the kingdom of God, and everything you need will be provided." That law of divine providence is more absolute than any physical law and is the basis for family security.

Gandhi

Dear Gandhi,

Now that you have the benefit of the hereafter, have you finally seen the light and become a Christian?

Praying for you,
Eve Angelist

Dear Eve,

I am still a Hindu, and Jesus is still a Jew. But some of our best friends are Christians, and we have all benefitted by your prayers.

Gratefully,
Gandhi

Dear Gandhi,

When we leaflet on one side of the white line at Bangor, we get arrested by Bangor base guards. When we leaflet on the other side of the white line, we get arrested by sheriff's deputies. Is there a solution to this problem?

Sincerely,
Ground Zero Activist

Dear GZA,

Better than that. There are three:
1) Paint everything white.
2) Take up skywriting.
3) Get the guards and deputies to leaflet.

Gandhi

Dear Gandhi,

I am the father of two teenagers who I'm convinced are on their way to hell from listening to rock and roll music. When I hear those awful drums beating and the voices of my children wailing, their hands clapping to the beat, I feel that Satan has taken over our home.

I've tried everything I could think of to free my kids from this demonic drumbeat music, from giving them tickets to the symphony (which they exchanged for seats at a rock concert) to playing my favorite Guy Lombardo records at dinner (which they respond to by plugging their ears and slurping their soup).

Gandhi, how can I deliver my ears and their souls from this hellish cacophony of rock?

Sincerely,
Ears Shocking from Kids Rocking

Dear Ears Shocking,

In the way you put it, this is a theological controversy: Heaven is the realm of swing and sway, and in hell the beat goes on. I am not sure that God has your ear for music.

Try head sets and heart open.

Gandhi

Dear Gandhi,

How can you profess such faith in nonviolence when it is clear that history teaches the opposite lesson? History is the story of war, oppression, inhumanity of all kinds. Please acknowledge that history is against you, and that in a world of the sword one must take up the sword for survival.

Sincerely,
Convinced by the Facts

Dear Convinced,

History is really a record of every interruption of the even working of the force of love or of the soul. Two brothers quarrel, one of them repents and re-awakens the love that was lying dormant in him; the two again begin to live in peace; nobody takes note of this. But if the two brothers, through the intervention of solicitors or for some other reason, take up arms or go to law—which is another form of the exhibition of brute force—their doings would be immediately noticed in the press, they would be the talk of their neighbors and would probably go down in history.

And what is true of families and communities is true of nations. There is no reason to believe that there is one law for families and another for nations. History, then, is a record of interruptions in the course of nature. Soul force, being natural, is not noted in history.

Gandhi*

Dear Gandhi,

In your response to "Convinced by the Facts," you point out that "history is a record of interruptions in the course of nature." I would like to put a little more responsibility on the shoulders of your correspondent.

There seems to be a built-in prejudice for evil in the human brain—or at least in the contemporary Western brain. One never sees a headline proclaiming "99.7% of the populace went to bed safely last night." It is only the unusual which grabs our attention.

Thus "Convinced by the Facts" is paying attention to only a few of the facts. What's more, we all find what we're looking for. If you assume that the human being is anti-social, uncooperative, and negative, you will find plenty of supporting evidence. Similarly, if you assume that the human being is a social creature, and that the only way which our ancestors over a million years were able to survive was through cooperation, then you'll find plenty of evidence for that view.

The rational reason for making the second assumption is that the first one can lead only to the annihilation of life on this planet. The second assumption, although not guaranteeing survival, does give us the most promising basis for acting to insure survival.

And besides, it's a lot more fun living.

Love and peace,
Igal Roodenko

Dear Igal,

I have shared your letter with "Convinced by the Facts," who has decided that the course of prudence is to join the War Resisters League. What convinced "Convinced" was your final sentence.

Gandhi

Dear Gandhi,

You have been selected by our computer to receive a free dessert with any meal served on our premises within the next three months. When can we expect to see you at one of our tables?

Sincerely,
Steak House

Dear Steak House,

When the cows give their consent.

Gandhi

Dear Gandhi,

I listen to a lot of preachers, teachers, and politicians. They talk about morality, and how we need more of it. But they all seem to be talking about different things. How can I tell what is moral, and what if I disagree with them about it? What if "moral" action produces no results?

Sincerely,
List Ning

Dear List,

How can you understand morality if you do not use your own intelligence and power of thought, but let yourself be swept along like a log of wood by the current? Television preachers or politicians aren't enough. What we need is to see that the act is good and is done with a good intention. It must be done without compulsion, without self-interest, and for the common good. Then an action is moral. It may be that we do not actually see good results flowing from the action: The result of an action is not within our command. God alone gives fruits.

Gandhi*

Dear Gandhi,

I read that after President Reagan's last press conference, which provided no news, the Senate Minority Leader telephoned him to say, "Mr. President, you hit it out of the park." What was that supposed to mean?

Sincerely,
Curious Citizen

Dear Citizen,

The batter who hits a baseball out of the park is entitled to run around the bases without being tagged. Hitting one out of the park is therefore a successful run-around. The Senate Minority Leader's words were well-chosen.

Gandhi

Dear Gandhi,

As a fellow statesman and student of history, I would like to point out that anything you accomplished ignored the reality of power. I find your life somewhat irresponsible in that regard. From your present, presumably more objective viewpoint, would you please acknowledge that our destinies are in fact ruled by power.

With all due respect,
H. Kissinger

Dear Mr. Kissinger,

I think the power you speak of should be taken with a grain of salt.

Gandhi

Dear Gandhi,

When the Department of Energy repainted the White Train, they painted its sides blue, green, brown, red, and charcoal grey but kept the top of the cars white. The DOE admits that they painted over the white sides because the train had become so visible—and they must mean visible to us U.S. citizens, who are the ones who see the train from the side when it goes through our towns and who line the tracks to say "No" to it.

But because the train remains white on top, it is just as easy to spot today from a Soviet spy satellite as it was before.

Gandhi, what about the Russians? Isn't the DOE concerned about them following the train?

Sincerely,
Puzzled Train Watcher

Dear Puzzled,

The White Train as a component of U.S. nuclear policy must fulfill a complex purpose.

It must simultaneously (a) deter the Soviet Union from attacking the United States, (b) in the meantime, prepare a first strike build-up of U.S. forces against the Soviet Union, and (c) keep U.S. citizens from noticing nuclear weapons at all.

The White Train by being highly visible on top (to the Soviet military), camouflaged on the sides (to U.S. citizens), and loaded secretly in the Pantex Plant (with first strike weapons) corresponds to the complex purpose of U.S. nuclear policy.

A fourth factor in White Train shipments, the danger of derailment, expresses the degree of sanity in this policy.

Gandhi

Dear Gandhi,

I am a judge with my heart in the right place. I am now getting cases of Trident protesters who claim that international law condemning nuclear weapons is the supreme law of the land. These protesters tell me to read the United States Constitution, the Nuremberg Principles, the United Nations Charter, and other esoteric documents.

However, in law school nobody told me to do that. They told me to read case law, and I am not finding any case law that says that condemning our national defense policies is the supreme law of the land.

What do you advise me to read, Gandhi? What do you advise me to do?

Sincerely,
Jack Justice

Dear Jack,

I went to law school, too. I suggest that you read the law of love in your own heart and apply that to the case before you. You will find the documents you need.

Gandhi

Dear Gandhi,

How many people are needed to go on the tracks to stop the White Train in its path?

Sincerely,
R. Dent Organizer

Dear R. Dent,

If it is the engineer who decides for reasons of conscience to leave the train and go on the tracks, then no one else is needed to stop the train.

If it is instead just one satyagrahi on the tracks, but with enough love in her or his heart to reach the people responsible for the train, there is still only one person needed.

A few people who love their opponents deeply can stop the train more easily than thousands who have resentment and hatred in their hearts.

Gandhi

Dear Gandhi,

I am a rock-and-roll recording artist. I have been asked to record a theme song for the TV situation comedy based on your life which has been inspired by the movie, *Gandhi*. As the show begins, you will be shown walking into jail. Do you have any suggestions for my accompanying song?

Sincerely,
Rock Against Violence

Dear Rock,

How about "See You Later, Agitator"?

Gandhi

Dear M. K. Gandhi,

You are invited to apply for a loan of $3,500 or more from the privacy of your home...with a speed, ease, and convenience that will surprise you, M. K. Gandhi.

If you've ever been frustrated with long, detailed, time-consuming applications, you can now forget about that extra paperwork, M. K. Gandhi. Our financial services make it quick and easy for you to apply for $3,500 or more.

We pay the postage, and we do the paperwork. We're sure you'll agree that this is the most convenient way to apply for the money you want, M. K. Gandhi. We look forward to receiving your request.

Sincerely,
Home Loan Services

Dear Home Loan Services,

I request that you return to your borrowers all the interest you have extracted from them, that you give your capital freely and promptly to people in need, and that you enroll your computer in a creative writing course.

Gandhi

Dear Gandhi,

I recently won a gold medal as a sprinter in the Olympics. Now I would like to adapt my talent to the field of satyagraha. Please tell me how I can become a person of nonviolence in the fastest time.

Sincerely,
Doris Dash

Dear Doris,

The fastest way is to slow down.

Gandhi

Dear Gandhi,

I have been going to a lot of demonstrations lately, and I always go intending to be nonviolent. When I get there I see counter-demonstrators. Yesterday at Cape Canaveral's anti-Trident rally there was an airplane trailing a sign that said, "A little nukie never hurt anyone!" When I see things like this I get so angry. How can we hope to achieve change when these people are so gross and insensitive?? It seems hopeless to me!

Sincerely,
Peace Walker

Dear Peace,

First, congratulations on having gone to the Cape to express your views. But consider this: The force of love only truly comes into play when it meets with the causes of hatred. True nonviolence does not ignore or blind itself to the causes of hatred, but in spite of the knowledge of their existence, operates upon the person setting those causes in motion. The law of nonviolence—returning good for evil, loving one's enemy—involves a knowledge of the blemishes of the "enemy." Hence do the Scriptures say, "Forgiveness is an attribute of the brave." Join me in working to forgive.

Gandhi*

Dear Gandhi,

You used to live with co-workers on the charity of friends who defrayed the expenses of your ashram. Nowadays Catholic Workers do that, too, and some of the people involved in peace groups. Do you think it proper for a group of able-bodied people to live on the charity of friends?

Sincerely,
Indignant

Dear Indignant,

You have taken the word "charity" too literally. You should understand that the members of such a group give their bodies and their minds to its work. The group can still be said to live on the charity of friends because the latter get no direct return for their donations. The fruits of the labor go to the cause of peace.

Gandhi*

Dear Gandhi,

I have read an article saying we can only resist out of love. I find I can't dump my burdens of fear and anger, though I do feel the love power. Can I do peace work?

Sincerely,
Impure

Dear Imp,

Come as you are. Maybe we can work out a peace conversion for your hitch-hiking friends.

Gandhi

Dear Gandhi,

I have just taken up the hobby of hang-gliding. The other day when I strapped on my wings and jumped off a cliff for the first time, I hit an up-draft and started going up. Unfortunately before jumping off, I forgot to learn how to go down in a situation like this.

Gandhi, it is now two days later and I am still gliding up and the clouds are far below. You will notice from my envelope that your address is hastily scribbled with my stamp a bit askew. But I am trusting that someone down there will pick up this letter of distress and mail it to you quickly. Gandhi, I keep going higher and higher! What force of truth can bring me down to earth? What should I do?

Sincerely,
Icarus Americanus

Dear Icarus,

You forgot to put down your return address.

Gandhi

Dear Gandhi,

Since there is only one God, should there not be only one religion?

Sincerely,
I Found It

Dear Found It,

This is a strange question. Just as a tree has a million leaves, similarly, though God is one, there are as many religions as there are men and women, though they are all rooted in one God. We do not see this plain truth because we are followers of different prophets and claim as many religions as there are prophets.

Gandhi*

Dear Gandhi,

I have noticed that people in the government are now identifying our enemies in Grenada, Lebanon, and wherever they are found as "thugs." Thinking this an important change from "communists" and "terrorists" as the enemy to be destroyed, I looked up "thug" in the dictionary. It says a thug is "a member of a former religious organization in India who murdered and robbed in the service of Kali, a god of destruction; hence any assassin, cutthroat, or ruffian."

Thugs definitely sound like a danger. What threat do you think there is, Gandhi, of thugs taking over the world?

Sincerely,
A Citizen Against Thugs

Dear Citizen,

Thugs seem to be on the increase both at home and abroad wherever there is a possibility of crime in the streets, which can happen whenever there are people in the streets. The government is suggesting that we will have no more thugs when there are no more people in the streets, or simply no more people.

I think the god of destruction should be taken seriously.

Gandhi

Dear Gandhi,

Have a little question for you. Saw a quote from Robert McAfee Brown that says:

What you listen to is what you hear.

Where you stand is what you see.

What you do is what you are.

I do a lot of time. Am I a timer?

Carl Kabat
Huntingdon State Prison

Dear Carl,

Time will tell.

Gandhi

Editors' note: Since writing this question, Carl Kabat has continued to do a lot of time for his peacemaking. He is currently serving an 18-year prison sentence at the federal prison in Milan, Michigan for the Silo Pruning Hooks disarmament action.

Dear Gandhi,

I have been reading reports on Archbishop Raymond Hunthausen, who seems to advocate unilateral disarmament. What can he (and you) be thinking of?? If we put down our weapons we'll be the laughingstock of the world, and vulnerable to any kind of attack and blackmail!

Sincerely,
Not Laughing

Dear Not,

Don't be too sure! Unless the world is to commit suicide, some nation will have to dare to disarm herself and take large risks. The level of nonviolence in that nation will naturally have risen so high as to command universal respect. Her judgements will be unerring, her decisions will be firm, her capacity for heroic self-sacrifice will be great, and she will want to live as much for other nations as herself. That doesn't mean she will be defenseless. Investigate some of the work currently being done by people like Gene Sharp to develop methods of nonviolent civilian defense.

Gandhi*

Dear Gandhi,

I am sending you and *Ground Zero* a pocket computer game called "Overcoming Trident." The game is programmed with all the political factors that are involved in the actual campaign to stop Trident. I have played this game myself over 4,000 times without winning. I thought this dose of reality might help you folks to see the world for what it is.

Sincerely,
Hy Tech

Dear Hy,

Your computer can't program Love. I suggest that we all refuse to play that game.

Gandhi

Dear Gandhi,

As a professional boxer I have won twenty-seven fights in a row, twenty-six by knockouts. However, after seeing the movie "Gandhi" on TV and then reading your works, I have realized that my profession is brutal, immoral, and unjustifiable. Instead of a professional boxer, I now wish to be a satyagrahi committed to the end of violence in this country and the world.

In order to share my conversion to nonviolence with the largest possible audience, I plan to announce this change of direction at the beginning of the first round of my scheduled fight for the heavyweight championship of the world. As the bell rings and the champion advances toward me from his corner, I shall take off my gloves, throw them in the center of the ring, and walk toward my opponent with my hands extended in friendship.

What is your advice, Gandhi, for the next steps in my life?

Sincerely,
The Real Rocky Balboa

Dear Rocky,

Don't trip over your gloves.

Gandhi

Dear Gandhi,

I have invented a new labor-saving device that will make thousands of workers happy as they will not have to work. Someone has told me that you are against machinery. I am a good Gandhian and I want to know why. What's wrong with machines?

Sincerely,
Pat Ent

Dear Pat,

What I object to is the craze for machinery, not machinery as such. The craze is for what you call "labor-saving" machinery. We go on saving labor until thousands are without work and thrown on the open streets to die of starvation. Do you think they are happy? I want to save time and labor, not for a fraction of humankind, but for all. I want the concentration of wealth not in the hands of a few, but in the hands of all. Today, machinery merely helps a few to ride on the backs of millions. The impetus behind it all is not the philanthropy to save labor, but greed. It is against this constitution of things that I am fighting with all my might.

Gandhi*

Dear Gandhi,

We are parents who believe in nonviolence and abhor nuclear weapons. Yet our teenage son and daughter both say they want to join the Navy and serve on the USS *Ohio*. We keep giving them the right kind of books to read, taking them to the best peace lectures, etc. Now they're talking about applying to the U.S. Naval Academy! What did we do wrong?

Sincerely,
Mom and Dad Who've Been Had

Dear Mom and Dad WBH,

I had the same kind of problem. None of my children turned out to be me. What you did wrong was to conceive your children with that kind of expectation.

Gandhi

Dear Gandhi,

I am appalled by cereal commercials which seduce children and adults into starting the day by eating garbage. In reality these excuses for nourishment are filled with sugar, air, and giveaway toys. I urge a return to good, old-fashioned porridge, which I eat every morning from a recipe handed down through generations which leaves both body and soul satisfied.

Sincerely,
Pull for Porridge

Dear Pull,

I congratulate you on having the porridge of your convictions.

Gandhi

Dear Gandhi,

I've been reading your books and I know that you consider the search for God to be the search for Truth, and thus our highest aim in life. What puzzles me is the frequency with which my understanding of God and God's truth is opposed to my parents' and friends' understandings. How can I defend my Truth, and what do I do to convince them they're wrong?

Sincerely,
Right

Dear Right,

What may appear as Truth to one person will often appear as untruth to another. That need not worry the seeker. Where there is an honest effort, it will be realized that what appear to be different truths are like the countless leaves of one tree. There is nothing wrong in every person following the truth according to his/her own lights. It is indeed our duty to do so. If there is a mistake on any of our parts, it will automatically be set right through self-suffering. In the search for truth we cannot lose our bearing for wrong—directly we take to the wrong path we stumble and are thus directed to the right one.

Gandhi*

Dear Gandhi,

I'm coming to you as a court of last resort on a question of civil disobedience. I'm confused as to why the media treats Martin Luther King as a hero and Colonel Oliver North as a criminal. Even granting what I don't grant in the case of Oliver, isn't it true that both men disobeyed the law for the sake of a higher cause?

Sincerely,
Patrick Buchanan

Dear Patrick,

Yes, but Martin Luther King's cause was higher than the next floor.

Gandhi

Dear Gandhi,

This is Patrick again. That was a pretty cute answer for a saint, but if you're going to justify law-breaking by higher-than-thou causes, isn't that the end justifying the means? And doesn't that notorious principle contradict nonviolence?

Your old friend,
Patrick Buchanan

Dear Patrick,

Thank you for your faithful correspondence. Besides the differences in ends, Martin's means or violations of the law were done in an open, nonviolent way while respecting and communicating with his opponents. In terms of our final impact on history, he or she who means well ends well.

Gandhi

Dear Gandhi,

I am a rattlesnake. I know no other way of life. I realize that a number of people are startled by me. How can I convince them that I am nothing more than a simple serpent sincerely seeking peace?

Sincerely,
Rhonda Rattler

Dear Rhonda,

You are adding to your problem. Simple serpents don't write letters. If you must write, at least use less s's. It reads like hissing.

Gandhi

Dear Gandhi,

I am writing to question *Ground Zero*'s recurring statement that Trident has a first strike capability. So what? Every weapon or potential weapon has a first strike capability. That includes spears, bows and arrows, slingshots, spitballs, and my Aunt Sally's dishes (if she decides to throw them). If a first strike capability is such a big deal, is *Ground Zero* also against my Aunt Sally's dishes?

Sincerely,
First Strike Skeptic

Dear First,

The Circular Error Probability of Aunt Sally's dishes does qualify each of them as a first strike weapon. Their ability to destroy hardened Soviet missile silos does not. You and Aunt Sally can read First Strike! *by Robert C. Aldridge (South End Press, 116 St. Botolph Street, Boston, MA 02115 $9.00 plus $1.50 postage) to clarify what the U.S. and Soviet Union are prepared to dish out.*

Gandhi

Dear Gandhi,

I have read enough of your writing to know that you are against bloodshed. But when I watched the civil rights movement on TV and when I saw the movie about your life, it was clear that nonviolent action can result in bloodshed. How can you go on advocating it when you know the results?

Sincerely,
Squeamish

Dear Squeamish,

As I have often stated, what strikes me down is not the sight of blood under every conceivable circumstance. It is blood spilled by the noncooperators or their supporters in breach of their declared vows which paralyzes me as it ought to paralyze every honest noncooperator.

Gandhi*

Dear Gandhi,

I'm having terrible problems with truth and diplomacy. No matter what I say I'm not believed, and people keep finding out more and more of my secret policy. You did a wonderful job of maintaining your image and your credibility. Can you tell me your secret weapon? Quick!!

In haste,
R. Reagan

Dear R.R.,

I have no secret methods. I know no diplomacy save that of truth. I have no weapons but nonviolence. I may be unconsciously led astray for awhile, but not for all time. My commitment to truth is well-defined self-limitation. And when I make a mistake, I admit it—and change my ways.

Gandhi*

Dear Gandhi,

I am one of a number of large flatfish found in northern seas which are known to the human species as "halibut." For some reason people are fond of catching and eating us, even those people who don't eat the flesh of animals. This is a distinction which no doubt has its reasons but which we fish find it somewhat hard to appreciate.

Gandhi, I want to express my appreciation to you for a life in which you not only did not eat animals or fish of any kind but also suggested alternative diets to others.

Sincerely,
Helen Halibut

Dear Helen,

In your case I did it just for the halibut.

Gandhi

Dear Gandhi,

I hear a lot about the so-called "religious peace movement" these days—the Christian and Jewish and even Buddhist peace groups are getting a lot of coverage. After all the thousands of bloody years of religious history, how can anybody look to religion for peace? Religious people have instituted more violence, crusades, pogroms, holy wars, etc., than just about anybody else. How can people seriously talk about God and peace?

Sincerely,
Disgusted

Dear Disgusted,

True religion being the greatest thing in life and in the world, has been exploited the most. And those who have seen the exploiters and the exploitation and missed the reality naturally get disgusted with the thing itself. But religion is after all a matter for each individual and then too a matter of the heart. Call it then by whatever name you like, that which gives one the greatest solace in the midst of the severest fire is God.

Gandhi*

Dear Gandhi,

You have the reputation of never being angry. Is that true? Are you human?

Sincerely,
Ida Wonder

Dear Ida,

It is not that I do not get angry, but that I do not give vent to anger. I cultivate the quality of patience as angerlessness, but I can only control my anger when it comes. How I find it possible to control anger would be a useless question, for it is a habit that everyone must form for him or herself. Anger is part of the human condition, and I most certainly am human!

Gandhi*

Dear Gandhi,

I know that you urged satyagrahis to eliminate all fear from their hearts. I plan to be in a Peace Blockade boat this summer, yet find that I am not totally without fear when I think of the Trident submarine bearing down upon us. What do you recommend?

Sincerely,
Still a Little Scared

Dear Still,

A life preserver.

Gandhi

Dear Gandhi,

Will you please explain how you could ever have said anything so stupid as the following:

"I do not consider Hitler to be as bad as he is depicted. He is showing an ability which is amazing and he seems to be gaining his victories without much bloodshed."

Sincerely,
Anti-Fascist

Dear Anti-Fascist,

I made many mistakes in my life, and clearly this opinion of Hitler was a mistaken one. However, I believe that my diagnosis of the challenge posed by Hitler was an accurate one:

"Democracy dreads to spill blood. The philosophy for which Hitler and Mussolini stand calls it cowardice to shrink from bloodshed. They exhaust the resources of poetic art in order to glorify organized murder. There is no humbug about their word or deed. They are ever ready for war. There is nobody in Germany or Italy to cross their path. Their word is law.

"But a democracy cannot maintain itself on a perpetual war footing and remain a democracy. Science of war leads one to dictatorship pure and simple. Science of nonviolence alone can lead to pure democracy. England, France, and the United States have to make their choice; that is the challenge of the two dictators." (October 15, 1938)

I believe your history is bearing out my words.

Gandhi*

Dear Gandhi,

I think world leaders should take up surfing as the way to overcome war. Man, riding those big waves under open skies will give anybody a high that makes power trips dissolve into bubbles. If I could do it, I'd make surfing the order of the day for every national bigwig. Then you'd see peace fly like never before. Ride the waves, Gandhi. Be a surfing satyagrahi, man.

Aloha, skinny bro,
Surfin Bliss

Dear Surfin,

Some countries have the misfortune to have no surf. Others with surf have leaders unable to get aboard surf boards or stay upright on them for any length of time even if you should become their Secretary of Surf.

But I welcome the vision of leaders having to negotiate their differences on the beach with nothing more to shield them from world opinion than their bathing suits. If they were to try out the surf, maybe they would also realize that they sink or swim together.

Gandhi

Dear Gandhi,

I am a strict vegetarian. Should I allow my dog to eat meat?

Sincerely,
Seeking Consistency

Dear Seeking,

Let your canine be your guide.

Gandhi

Dear Gandhi,

What action is key to overcoming a state that is preparing for nuclear war?

Sincerely,
Ann Alyst

Dear Ann,

The lock of the nuclear state is nothing more than your own cooperation with it. What key in your life can your heart and mind find to open that lock to peace?

Gandhi

Dear Gandhi,

Why did you remain silent for one day of every week? Wasn't that a bit of a nuisance in the midst of all your responsibilities?

Sincerely,
Chatter Matters

Dear Chatter,

Silence has now become both a physical and spiritual necessity for me. Originally it was taken to relieve the sense of pressure. Then I wanted time for writing. After, however, I had practiced it for some time, I saw the spiritual value of it. It suddenly flashed across my mind that that was the time when I could best hold communion with God. And now I feel as though I was created for silence. A seeker after truth has to be silent.

Gandhi*

Dear Gandhi,

I am an ice cream vendor and want to put my vocation at the service of the peace movement. I would like to follow the route of the Nuclear Train so that I can provide refreshment to vigilers by the tracks. Will you please tell me where I should station my Good Humor truck so that I'll be in the right place at the right time. Warmer states are more appropriate if you have those available.

Sincerely,
Gladys Good Humor

Dear Gladys,

The Nuclear Train has traveled from the Pantex Plant in Amarillo, Texas to Bangor, Washington, or more frequently now, to Charleston, South Carolina where the climate tends to be balmier. However, even in warmer places by the tracks your services may not be required. The sight of the Nuclear Train is chilling enough.

Gandhi

Dear Gandhi,

You used your methods of noncooperation to rid India of a conqueror. Are such methods compatible with the plight of draft refusers and other activists in the United States?

Sincerely,
Refusing

Dear Refusing,

As a member of a subject nation I could best help by shaking myself rid of my subjection. But here I am asked how best to get out of a military mentality. You are enjoying your amenities on condition that you render military service to the state. There you have to get the state rid of its military mentality.

Noncooperation in military service and service in non-military matters are not compatible. "Refusing" military service is an ill-chosen word. You are all the while giving military service by deputy because you are supporting a state which is based on military service. In some countries people are exempted from military service, but they still have to pay money to the state. You will have to extend the scope of your noncooperation to your taxes.

Gandhi*

Dear Gandhi,

I deliver newspapers and have noticed that the newspaper I distribute presents a very biased and negative view of the world.

To rectify that situation, I have decided to insert the *Ground Zero* newspaper periodically in the paper I deliver. I believe this step will help to balance the bad news with the good news and create a better-informed citizenry.

Sincerely,
Billy Batson

Dear Billy,

Please try not to put Ground Zero *in the comics, sports section, or obituaries, which will just confuse matters. How about the classifieds?* Ground Zero *members are already wanted for a variety of reasons.*

Gandhi

Dear Gandhi,

I am a deer living on the Trident submarine base at Bangor. I feel caught in a strange situation. Because the base is a game preserve, my family and I are safer here than we are outside the base fence where we fear being shot. But I am uneasy in this fenced-in home when I see the "No Hunting" signs near the Explosives Handling Wharf, where hundreds of hydrogen bombs are loaded into Trident submarines and aimed at millions of people. Are we deer safe, Gandhi, only where the people hunt people instead?

Sincerely,
Fenced-In Bambi

Dear Bambi,

Your safety and that of all the earth's creatures remains dependent on the self-endangered species which has fenced you in. For the sake of all life, it is time for us humans to renounce human hunting.

Gandhi

Dear Gandhi,

I am a young businessman and I have eleven dependents. I believe in truth and nonviolence but find I cannot strictly follow it in business. What should I do? Abandoning the business means suffering for my relations.

Sincerely,
John Mercantile

Dear John,

This begs the question. It is difficult but not impossible to conduct strictly honest business. What is true is that honesty is incompatible with amassing a large fortune.

Gandhi*

Dear Gandhi,

I want to do something for the cause of peace through nonviolence, but when I begin to take action I always find that other things in my life get in the way. There is always something more important that comes up. What do I do about this?

Sincerely,
Busy

Dear Busy,

My friend Arthur Harvey has recently written some critical comments about your American peace movement that might be of some help to you. Arthur writes:

"Real nonviolence conflicts with prosperity. It threatens our security both psychological and material, but I refer especially to money, property, a successful career. Even in a time when security has lost much of its former assurance, people still cling to the residue. Young people often want to take a risk for the sake of good, but draw back when it begins to threaten their financial future.

"The anti-nuclear movement has attracted thousands of people. Most have been burned out and demoralized after one arrest. It works this way: The new recruit responds to a strongly worded call to action. Little or nothing is required in the way of preparation or commitment. In due course he or she is arrested and charged with trespass or whatever. At this point s/he suddenly remembers an English exam s/he must take in a few days. The leaders of the action, understanding his/ her predicament, arrange through a friendly lawyer to have the court process postponed or settled by paying a fine and/or agreeing not to repeat the offense. One might look at all this as merely legal gobbledegook, but it also demoralizes a beginning effort by people trying to make a serious stand for good and against evil."

Gandhi

Editors' note: Arthur Harvey is a nonviolent activist who writes thoughtful and provocative letters on Gandhian nonviolence. You may wish to write him c/o Greenleaf Books, Canton, Maine to request copies of his letters. You will not always agree with him, but he will make you think hard!

Dear Gandhi,

When I was in Geneva recently, the President of the United States told me he wished our planet were threatened by an alien invader so that our peoples could unite in response to it. I was too stunned for a reply. Can you help me?

Sincerely,
Mikhail Gorbachev

Dear Mikhail,

The alien invader to life on earth is the attitude that any people's security can be based on nuclear weapons.

Gandhi

Dear Gandhi,

Who is your choice in the United States presidential election?

Sincerely,
George Gallup

Dear George,

If he were to run, I would vote for Winston Churchill. Winston is remembered well by the people of your country, and he has now given up cigars, war, and imperialism. Perhaps you can find a candidate there who has done the same.

Gandhi

Dear Gandhi,

When I talk with people who disagree with me on the question of nuclear weapons, I sometimes find myself getting very angry at them. When I'm leafletting the Trident base, I find that some people get very angry at me—calling names, driving their cars at me, etc. Do you think this kind of hostility is acceptable?

Sincerely,
E.Z. Doesit

Dear E.Z.,

The golden rule of conduct is mutual toleration, seeing that we will never all think alike and we shall see Truth in fragment and from different angles of vision. Conscience is not the same thing for all. Therefore differences of opinion should never mean hostility. If they did, my wife and I should be sworn enemies of one another. I do not know two persons in the world who had no differences of opinion, and as I am a follower of the Gita, I have always attempted to regard those who differ from me with the same affection as I have for my nearest and dearest.

Gandhi*

Dear Gandhi,

I am a vegetarian by belief but I have found that I don't particularly like vegetables. As a matter of fact, I prefer chocolate milkshakes to vegetables. I have seen the movie *Gandhi*, and was impressed by the fact that you drank no chocolate milkshakes. Does that mean I should change my ways and become the kind of vegetarian who not only eats vegetables but abstains from milkshakes?

Sincerely,
Puzzled Palate

Dear Puzzled P.,

The reason I drank no milkshakes in the film is that Ben Kingsley was on a diet so that he would look more like me.

Gandhi

Dear Gandhi,

I have been imprisoned by my cruel master, Stromboli, for refusing to cooperate with his exploitative puppet show. Now that I am in jail, can you give me some guidance on how to behave?

Sincerely,
Pinocchio

Dear Pinocchio,

As noncooperators we must work in the jails, for we do not normally noncooperate with the jails. We submit to the court's discipline when we are taken to a trial. Civil disobedience by its very nature requires us to yield complete obedience to jail regulations, for as civil resisters we invite imprisonment and are bound to suffer the rigors of discipline.

But we can civilly resist such regulations as are not only irksome or hard to bear but are humiliating or specially designed to degrade noncooperators. Our self-respect demands willing obedience to jail discipline. The same self-respect may require resistance to misbehavior euphemistically called discipline. For instance, we would refuse to draw lines with our noses whether within or without jail.

Gandhi*

Dear Gandhi,

The more I read about your life, the more conscious I am that you were an incredibly strong personality, able to carry on when all around you opposed what you were doing. I, on the other hand, am just a normal person with a great desire to be liked—but also a great desire to do good. What was your greatest strength, and how did you achieve it?

Sincerely,
Em U. Lator

Dear Em,

I was conscious of my own limitations. That consciousness was my only strength. Whatever I might have been able to do in my life proceeded more than anything else out of the realization of my own limitations. That is a great strength you have as well!

Gandhi

Dear Gandhi,

A local radio station claims in a recent survey that 98% of the people in Kitsap County support Trident. Where does that leave *Ground Zero?*

Sincerely,
Curious George

Dear George,

In the minority.

Gandhi

Dear Gandhi,

Did you have any particular teacher on nonviolence?

Sincerely,
Guru Researcher

Dear GR,

I learned the lesson of nonviolence from my wife, when I tried to bend her to my will. Her determined resistance to my will on the one hand, and her quiet submission to the suffering my stupidity involved on the other, ultimately made me ashamed of myself and cured me of my stupidity in thinking that I was born to rule over her, and in the end she became my teacher in nonviolence.

Gandhi*

Dear Gandhi,

I have been studying science and philosophy for many years, and I find that all the faith I had when I was a child has vanished. In grade school I was taught the proofs for the existence of God, but in college I learned that the proofs were false. I find that I no longer have faith.

Sincerely,
D. Thomas

Dear D.,

That is due to the fact that for you faith is an effort of the intellect, not an experience of the soul. Intellect takes us along in the battles of life to a certain limit, but at the crucial moment it fails us. Faith transcends reason. It is when the horizon is the darkest and human reason is beaten down to the ground that faith shines brightest and comes to our rescue. It is such faith that you require, and this comes when one has shed all pride of intellect and surrendered oneself entirely to God's will.

Gandhi*

Dear Gandhi,

It is known that you followed the practice of shaving. Isn't shaving an act of violence to one's natural growth of beard?

Sincerely,
Smith Brothers

Dear Smith Brothers,

In shaving I was disciplining the ambition of the hairs on my face to move upward from their natural roots. They accepted this discipline by offering their heads to my razor while retaining the life and freedom to grow more the next day, which they invariably did.

Gandhi

Dear Gandhi,

We are appalled at the popularity of recent violence-pandering movies which spawn an infinite number of sequels like *Rambo II* and *Rocky IV*. A nonviolent counterpoint is urgently needed as an antidote. Considering the acclaim received by your first film, do you have any plans in the works for *Gandhi II*, *Gandhi III*, *Gandhi IV*, etc.?

Hopefully,
Free People

Editors' note: Free People is the Tyler, Texas publisher of Both Sides Now, *a very occasional alternative magazine with Green leanings.*

Dear Free People,

As you know, my involvement in the Gandhi film consisted only in my living the life on which the film was based. Gandhi *the movie, like my life, ended with the death and cremation of Gandhi the man. Since that life, I have been a waitress in a vegetarian restaurant in Camden, New Jersey.* Gandhi II *would be* Margaret Jones. *So far, Richard Attenborough and Ben Kingsley haven't discovered me.*

Gandhi II *will be based on the transforming example which your lives are as capable of giving as mine is. I look forward to seeing that film.*

Gandhi

Dear Gandhi,

Why did you resort to a fast when you were faced with extreme difficulties? What effect does this have on the life of the public?

Sincerely,
Fast Relief

Dear F.R.,

Fasting is never intended to affect another's body. It must affect the heart. Hence it is related to the soul.

It is the last weapon of ahimsa. When human ingenuity fails, the votary fasts. This fasting quickens the spirit of prayer, that is to say, the fasting is a spiritual act.

Fasting is not to pressure a change because most things done under pressure of the fast have been undone after the fast is over. The fast expects only a cleansing of the heart.

Gandhi*

Dear Gandhi,

A problem I have as a baseball player is that I am addicted to chewing nervously on cherries when I come to bat. Often when the pitcher winds up, I'm spitting out my cherry pit and I end up swinging high and striking out. What should I do to improve my batting average?

Sincerely,
Johnny Strikeout

Dear Johnny,

Swing low, eat cherry pit.

Gandhi

Dear Gandhi,

I am striving hard to practice nonviolence, which I understand that you call ahimsa. I do not hit anyone, or cause any physical violence. Lately I have been having trouble understanding how to interact with others: police during demonstrations, President Reagan, etc. Some friends of mine say that it's still nonviolent to insult these folks as long as I don't use physical force against them. What do you think? Sometimes I really feel insulting!!

Sincerely,
No Hitter

Dear No,

Ahimsa is not the crude thing it has been made to appear. Not to hurt any living thing is no doubt part of ahimsa. But it is its least expression. The principle of ahimsa is hurt by every evil thought, by undue haste, by lying, by hatred, by wishing ill to anybody— *including Ronald Reagan. No insults, if you strive for ahimsa!*

Gandhi

Dear Gandhi,

I am disturbed that nuclear war is beginning to get a bad press. I have read several articles now that question the idea of winning a nuclear war. This is a defeatist notion that is weakening our nation's will to prevail in the world. When you're right, you're going to win, and nuclear war is no exception. Righteousness will bear a nuclear victory. What do you think?

Sincerely,
Ann I. Elation

Dear Ann,

I think you're dead right.

Gandhi

Dear Gandhi,

Are there cobras in heaven?

Sincerely,
Ecumenical Theologian

Dear Ecumenical,

That question strikes my fancy.

Gandhi

Dear Gandhi,

In deciding how to act, which is more important, the means or the end?

Sincerely,
Tentative

Dear Tentative,

There is such a close connection between the means and the end that it is difficult to say which of the two is more important. Or we may say that the means is the body and the end is the soul. The end is invisible, the means is visible. Now we have the pleasure in life of exploring this great truth.

Gandhi*

Dear Gandhi,

Is your "soul-force" attainable by the ignorant masses?

Sincerely,
A. Snob

Dear Snob,

They have it already in abundance. Once upon a time, an expedition of French scientists set out in search of knowledge and in due course reached India. They tried hard to find wisdom, as they expected, among the learned ones, but failed. Instead they found it in the home of an outcast Untouchable.

Gandhi*

Dear Gandhi,

Does God really look like George Burns?

Sincerely,
George Burns

Dear George,

No, like Gracie Allen. But She talks a lot like you.

Gandhi

Dear Gandhi,

Don't you think the nuclear arms race has made nonviolence passé? What in fact can the great powers of the world do, when they are threatened by their enemies with total destruction, except threaten counter-destruction for the sake of their own preservation?

Sincerely,
Peace Through Strength

Dear Peace Through Strength,

It is open to the great powers to take up nonviolence any day and cover themselves with glory and earn the eternal gratitude of posterity. If they or any of them can shed the fear of destruction, if they disarm themselves, they will automatically help the rest to regain their sanity. But then these great powers have to give up imperialistic ambitions and exploitation of the so-called uncivilized or semi-civilized nations of the earth and revise their mode of life. It means a complete revolution.

Great nations can hardly be expected in the ordinary course to move spontaneously in a direction the reverse of the one they have followed, and according to their notion of value, from victory to victory. But miracles have happened before and may happen even in this very prosaic age. Who can dare limit God's power of undoing wrong?

One thing is certain. If the mad race for armaments continues, it is bound to result in a slaughter such has never occurred in history. If there is a victor left, the very victory will be a living death for the nation that emerges victorious. There is no escape from the impending doom save through a bold and unconditional acceptance of the nonviolent method with all its glorious implications.

Gandhi*

Dear Gandhi,

I am a regular and enthusiastic reader of your column. In fact, I make copies to give to friends and relatives in order to convert them.

1) Is it all right to try to persuade people in this way?

2) Will I be arrested for violation of copyright laws?

Sincerely,
Avid Fan
(Helen Stritmatter)

Dear Avid,

I admire your efforts to convert people by this column. That is quite a task, and should teach you patience.

I think it would be appropriate to refer to your converts as "Dear Gandhiites." The conversion of someone by this column is a sign that anything can indeed happen in this world. Thus your Dear Gandhiite Movement has a hope and significance beyond numbers.

The only copyright law for "Dear Gandhi" is that you copy it right.

Gandhi

Dear Gandhi,

For the past 100 days I've had this craving for pizza, with no way to fulfill the lust. Did you ever use pizza in your experiments with truth?

Bemused behind bars,
Thornton Kimes

Dear Thornton,

Yes, my experiments began with the recognition that we all have a pizza the truth.

Gandhi

Editors' note: Thornton Kimes wrote his letter while serving a six-month jail sentence for cutting the fence at a missile silo in Conrad, Montana.

Dear Gandhi,

I want to commit civil disobedience against nuclear weapons. People keep telling me that I should get training and that I have to be committed to nonviolence. That seems like nonsense to me. What kind of training does it take to sit on *railroad tracks*????

Sincerely,
Ardent Activist

Dear Ardent,

Many people are playing at nonviolence. They think in terms of civil disobedience as meaning filling the jails. I must continue to repeat, even though it may cause nausea, that prison-going without the backing of honest constructive effort and good will in the heart for the wrong-doer is violence and therefore forbidden in satyagraha. Nonviolence is the decisive factor in civil disobedience. I have been told that people cannot be nonviolent overnight. I have never contended that they can. But I have held that by proper training they can become nonviolent, if they have the will. Active nonviolence is necessary for those who will offer civil disobedience.

Gandhi*

Dear Gandhi,

When I drive to work in the morning through heavy traffic, I have begun to question the way I act toward other drivers and pedestrians—cursing them, honking my horn, and waving my fist in the air. I have discovered that I am more nonviolent on the exercise machine in my own bedroom, where there are no other people in sight. But I can't get to work on my exercise machine.

Gandhi, how is it possible to drive an automobile without doing violence to other people, one's self, and the environment?

Sincerely,
Lost in Traffic

Dear Lost,

Try driving at walking speed, without a propellant which adds pollution to the air, and without the use of other materials which involve the exploitation of people or the earth. I am not sure if you can accomplish that task in an automobile but there are other means of transportation which are reliable in doing so. They require more use of the legs, less ambition in getting places, and will eliminate the need for your exercise machine.

Gandhi

Dear Gandhi,

What do you think of our state lottery?

Sincerely,
Gamblers for Social Responsibility

Dear GSR,

I do believe in a spinning wheel but one that is powered by freedom rather than greed.

Gandhi

Dear Gandhi,

I have so many needs and personal problems that I get confused and overwhelmed by the things I should be praying for. In this mass of needs, Gandhi, how should I pray?

Sincerely,
Seeking a Path

Dear Seeking,

There is really only one prayer that we may offer: "Thy will be done." That is to say, we do not wish to go where our wayward will may lead us but where the Lord takes us. We do not know whether it is good to live or die. Therefore we should not take delight in living, nor should we tremble at the thought of death. We should be equi-minded towards both. This is the ideal. It may be long before we reach it, and only a few of us can attain it. Even then we must keep it constantly in view, and the more difficult it seems of attainment, the greater should be the effort we put forth.

Gandhi*

Dear Gandhi,

Is there a particular truth at which satyagraha begins?

Sincerely,
Seeking the Source

Dear Seeking,

It is a fundamental principle of satyagraha that the tyrant whom the satyagrahi seeks to resist has power over one's body and material possessions, but can have no power over the soul. The soul can remain unconquered and unconquerable even when the body is imprisoned. The whole science of satyagraha was born from a knowledge of this fundamental truth.

Gandhi

Dear Gandhi,

If a people should ever be converted to nonviolence, how would they defend their country against aggression by another state?

Sincerely,
I. Deal Vision

Dear I. Deal,

If an aggressor invades such a society, there are two ways open to nonviolence.

First, to yield possession but noncooperate with the aggressor. Thus, supposing that a modern edition of Nero descended upon India, the representatives of the state will let him in but tell him that he will get no assistance from the people. They will prefer death to submission.

The second way would be nonviolent resistance by the people who have been trained in the nonviolent way. They would offer themselves unarmed as fodder for the aggressor's cannon.

The underlying belief in either case is that not even a Nero is devoid of a heart. The unexpected spectacle of endless rows upon rows of men and women simply dying rather than surrender to the will of an aggressor must ultimately melt him and his soldiers.

Such men and women will have shown personal bravery of a type far superior to that shown in armed warfare. In each case the bravery consists in dying, not in killing. There is no such thing as defeat in nonviolent resistance.

Gandhi*

Dear Gandhi,

When the elephants come out to do their tricks, I am the circus hand who cleans up after them with a shovel. I also take a keen interest in world events and am beginning to see my job as a symbol of God's task at the end of the world. I am wondering if this vision qualifies as theology.

Sincerely,
Roust About Truth

Dear Roust,

Yes, and physiology, too. You are on the track of a down-to-earth vision of the end. But remember that God may also be a clown and a high-wire artist.

Gandhi

Dear Gandhi,

I want to do my bit for peace, but I'm afraid that if I do I will eventually wind up in jail. The way things are going, I might not even have to choose civil disobedience. I might get put there for just watching trains. What do you think?

Sincerely,
Dis Inclined

Dear Dis,

Much though we have advanced in shedding fear of imprisonment, there is still a reluctance to seek it and an anxiety to avoid it. We must remain scrupulously honest and nonviolent, and at the same time be anxious almost to find ourselves in the jails of the government. It must be irksome to us to enjoy freedom under a government that we seek to end or mend. We must feel that we are paying some heavy price for maintaining our liberty. If therefore being innocent we are imprisoned, we must rejoice because we feel that freedom is near. Is not freedom nearer for the imprisonment of those who are now cheerfully undergoing it for the sake of peace and justice?

Gandhi*

Dear Gandhi,

Last night I had the strangest dream. I dreamed that there was another White Train carrying nuclear weapons from the place where they are made to the place where they would be put into missiles and lowered into submarines. This White Train traveled through cities and small towns and right through the center of our lives.

I dreamed that I was afraid because this White Train seemed so strong and untouchable and after all it was on a mission for our government transporting such implements of death for our protection against the enemy.

I dreamed that in my living room people gathered, and one by one as the house filled with people so did my heart fill with strength and love because I knew that we had joined together to prepare, to resist, and to say "no" to the White Train. I knew that in living rooms throughout those communities along the way of the White Train, others gathered to do the same, and I felt glad because I was not alone.

As we waited for the right moment to leave and go to where the train would be, I could feel the very positive energy and the Spirit descending and touching our lives, and the connections that were being made between all the people along the tracks. All the people included the train workers, the security personnel, the police, the weapons makers and, yes, all of God's creation.

Then the White Train changed its route to avoid us because the institutions which it represents are afraid of people's efforts to see the truth. I dreamed that each time the White Train appeared, more and more people turned out to witness the true nature of its mission, and more and more the train changed its route to avoid the people, and eventually there were no more routes to take.

Sincerely,
John Kefalas
Fort Collins, Colorado

Dear John,

Keep living that dream. More people are doing so. It is replacing a nightmare.

Gandhi

Dear Gandhi,

Do I have to be a Hindu to practice nonviolence? Or a Christian? It seems all the resisters I hear about here are Christians.

Sincerely,
Not One

Dear One,

Far be it from me to suggest that you should believe in the God that I believe in. Maybe your definition is different from mine, but your belief in that God must be your ultimate mainstay. It may be some supreme power or even a being indefinable, but belief in it is indispensable. To bear all kinds of torture without a murmur of resentment is impossible for a human being without the strength that comes from God. Only in God's strength are we strong. And only those who have faith can cast their cares and their fears on that immeasurable power.

Gandhi*
(Not one either)

Dear Gandhi,

I notice that in the annals of history it is considered great to sacrifice one's life for one's beliefs. Why should we not sacrifice the lives of others when necessary? The use of nuclear weapons, for example, requires a considerable human sacrifice; but would it not be justified if the reason were good enough?

Sincerely,
Willing

Dear Will,

Sacrifice of the lives of others cannot be justified on the grounds of necessity, for it is impossible to prove necessity. Sacrifice consists in suffering in one's own person so that others may benefit. Murder consists in making others suffer unto death so that the murderer, or those for whom s/he murders, may benefit.

Gandhi*

Dear Gandhi,

If you were somehow elected President of the United States, what would you do first?

Sincerely,
Polly T. Relevant

Dear Polly T.,

Resign.

Gandhi

Dear Gandhi,

Did you ever take out life insurance?

Sincerely,
Mutual of Omaha

Dear Mutual,

I did insure my life in 1901, and a short time after I gave up the policy because I felt I was distrusting God and making my relatives, in whose behalf the policy was taken, dependent upon me or the money I might leave them rather than upon God or themselves. The opinion arrived at when I gave up the policy has been confirmed by subsequent experience.

Gandhi*

Dear Gandhi,

How do you as a satyagrahi, a person of truth force, respond to defeat?

Sincerely,
Discouraged

Dear Discouraged,

Defeat has no place in the dictionary of nonviolence. The path of a satyagrahi is beset with insurmountable difficulties. But in true satyagraha there is neither disappointment nor defeat. As truth is all-powerful, satyagraha can never be defeated.

There is no time limit for a satyagrahi, nor is there a limit to the satyagrahi's capacity for suffering. Hence, there is no such thing as defeat in satyagraha. The so-called defeat may be the dawn of victory. It may be the agony of birth.

Gandhi*

Dear Gandhi,

I have noticed in your pictures that you did not have very good teeth. In fact you don't even seem to have very many of them. Do you have any suggestions to the young people of today on how to succeed in having better teeth than you did?

Sincerely,
Dental Distress

Dear Dental,

Brush your teeth faithfully after every meal, and work for a world in which meals are available to all. I have noticed that in certain parts of the world, the style of eating spawns and sustains dentists. I had more than enough teeth for the amount that I ate. You may require more.

Gandhi

Dear Gandhi,

If you had continued to be a would-be British gentleman practicing law, what would have happened to India?

Sincerely,
Spec Ulation

Dear Spec,

India would have remained west of China, south of Russia, and under a British boot.

Gandhi

Dear Gandhi,

I believe in nonviolence, but not as a form of masochism. How can I enlist in a nonviolent struggle without getting involved in suffering?

Sincerely,
Modest Hopes

Dear Modest,

According to the science of satyagraha, the greater the repression and lawlessness on the part of authority, the greater should be the suffering courted by the victims. Success is the certain result of suffering of the most extreme character, voluntarily undergone.

Peace or freedom won without sacrifice cannot last long. If you wish to contribute to genuine change, I suggest you get ready to make the highest sacrifice you are capable of. In true sacrifice all the suffering is on one side—one is required to master the art of getting killed without killing, of gaining life by losing it.

Gandhi*

Dear Gandhi,

Is the world getting better or worse?

Sincerely,
Wilma Whichway

Dear Wilma,

So long as I believe in a benevolent God, I must believe that the world is getting better even though I see evidence to the contrary.

Gandhi*

Dear Gandhi,

I am a dog whose owners have had difficulty in training me to "do my duty" outside the house. My mistress and master have tried countless methods to encourage me to go in what they regard as "the right place at the right time." All methods have failed. I have seen to that, and I wonder at this point why they persevere in trying. I really just prefer to go inside the house. I wish these otherwise intelligent people would recognize my right as an adult dog to make such a choice.

The question, Gandhi, is: How can I get my mistress and master to respect my right to select my own place of doing my business? Or is there any way to motivate myself to follow their preference? I fear it's just one more excuse for putting dogs in the back yard.

Sincerely,
Rags

Dear Rags,

Have you considered fasting as a way of appealing to your mistress and master? Besides the moral appeal, it would give them less to complain about. On the other hand, perhaps you could begin to enjoy the great outdoors more as a vacation spot and the garden as a fertile challenge.

Gandhi

Dear Gandhi,

History has shown nonviolence to be a costly and ineffective form of action. Now that the world is in such a terrible state, don't you think we should abandon nonviolence for a faster and more effective way of change? After all, we know where power really comes from.

Sincerely,
Em Sixteen

Dear Em,

The first thing you have to learn about history is that because something has not taken place in the past, does not mean it cannot take place in the future. Violence cannot bring an end to violence. All it can do is provoke violence. If we can adhere to complete nonviolence in thought, word, and deed, our freedom is assured.

Gandhi*

Dear Gandhi,

I am terrified of high places, and I work as a window washer at a downtown office building. My father and grandfather were also window washers, when the buildings were smaller. Because I never had the courage to confess to my family or employer my fear of heights, I kept going up in the business. Now I have an ulcer and am seeing a psychoanalyst during lunch breaks.

Gandhi, this is no small problem. I find even my psychoanalyst's couch a little high off the floor. Yet when I think of telling my father or my boss the truth after all these years, I get just as frightened as I do washing the highest window on a windy afternoon. I also can't give up my job because I need the salary and health benefits to pay my doctor bills. Any direction I go in life is terrifying: out of work, out on work, up, and especially down. What should I do?

Sincerely,
High and Dry

Dear High and Dry,

You are right in your assessment of high places, perhaps even of your psychoanalyst's couch: They do pose a risk, especially for you. However, the risk of not speaking the truth is greater.

Your predicament is not that unusual. It is like that of a defense worker or member of the armed services who has nightmares of killing people, yet is afraid to speak up in the daylight.

Gandhi

Dear Gandhi,

Is Gandhi the only thinker with a truth worth listening to?

Sincerely,
Phil Osopher

Dear Phil,

I ask nobody to follow me. Everyone should follow their own inner voice.

Gandhi*

Dear Gandhi,

I've been reading books about nonviolent civilian defense, and it seems to be a workable system, except for one thing. How can we defend our current economic system by nonviolence? The more I study, the more I find that we are exploiting weaker peoples for our own benefit. Surely that cannot be nonviolently defended! I think that economic justice would have to go hand in hand with disarmament. Do you agree?

Sincerely,
Broker

Dear Broker,

The principle of nonviolence necessitates complete abstention from exploitation in any form. If there were no greed, there would be no occasion for armament. Immediately the spirit of exploitation would be gone; armament would be felt as a positively unbearable burden. Real disarmament cannot come unless the nations of the world cease to exploit each other.

Gandhi*

Dear Gandhi,

People often kid me because of my appearance and way of walking. They say I look like I'm always wearing a tuxedo and that I wobble.

I'm becoming more sensitive to these remarks. I'm beginning to believe there's something wrong with the way I am. What do you think, Gandhi?

Sincerely,
Pete Penguin

Dear Pete,

I think you're all wet, and I love you for it.

Gandhi

Dear Gandhi,

I write a column similar to yours, as does my sister, Ann.

Gandhi, we have a proposal. How would you like to collaborate with the two of us in a "Dear Abby, Ann, and Gandhi" column? The dispersion of our energies in three directions seems such a waste when we could be working together—reconciled perhaps by gossipagraha?

What do you say, Mister G? The three of us together, syndicated, in lights, as it were?

Hopefully,
Abby

Dear Abby,

I feel a special responsibility to readers such as Rhonda Rattler, who are off the beaten path, and Pete Penguin, frozen off from ordinary discourse. I think your readers and my readers are sufficiently different for each of us to carry on in our respective paths. Besides, Ground Zero *won't release me from my contract.*

I wish you and Ann the very best.

Gandhi

Gandhi Bibliography

The best resource in the United States for Gandhi books is Greenleaf Books, Canton, Maine 04221, managed by Arthur Harvey. Write Greenleaf for their listing of hundreds of books by and about Gandhi, including used copies sold at reduced prices. All the books listed below except the Robert Payne biography are available from Greenleaf.

M. K. Gandhi, *An Autobiography or The Story of My Experiments in Truth* (Navajivan Publishing House: 1927). Covers Gandhi's life up to 1921; needs to be supplemented by his *Satyagraha in South Africa* and a good critical biography such as Ashe or Payne.

M. K. Gandhi, *Hind Swaraj or Indian Home Rule* (Navajivan Publishing House: 1938). His manifesto of nonviolent revolution, written in 1909 and held to all his life.

M. K. Gandhi, *The Message of Jesus Christ* (Bharatiya Vidya Bhavan: 1971). Gandhi's reverence for Jesus and rejection of Christianity should be considered by every searching Christian.

M. K. Gandhi, *Satyagraha* (Navajivan Publishing House: 1958). Comprehensive collection of Gandhi's writings on satyagraha or "truth-force."

M. K. Gandhi, *Satyagraha in South Africa* (Navajivan Publishing House: 1972). Absorbing account of the birth of satyagraha in Gandhi's South African campaigns.

Horace Alexander, *Gandhi Through Western Eyes* (New Society Publishers: 1984). Thoughtful portrait by a U.S. Quaker friend of Gandhi.

C.F. Andrews, *Mahatma Gandhi's Ideas* (George Allen & Unwin: 1930). Gandhi's vision presented by a loving, critical friend.

Geoffrey Ashe, *Gandhi* (Scarborough Books: 1980).

Joan Bondurant, *Conquest of Violence: The Gandhian Philosophy of Conflict* (University of California Press: 1965). Classic study of Gandhi's satyagraha campaigns by a political scientist.

Narayan Desai, *Growing Up With Gandhi* (Side 1); *Gandhian Training in Nonviolence* (Side 2). (Available from Theodore Herman, Cornwall Manor, Cornwall, PA 17016.) Cassette tape recording by one of Gandhi's foremost living disciples, who grew up in his ashram.

Eknath Easwaran, *Gandhi the Man* (Nilgiri Press: 1978). Beautiful introduction to the life and spirit of Gandhi, with many photos.

Robert Payne, *The Life and Death of Mahatma Gandhi* (E.P. Dutton: 1969).

Pyarelal, *Mahatma Gandhi*: Vol. I, *The Early Phase* (1869–96) (Navajivan Publishing House: 1965); Vol. II, *The Discovery of Satyagraha* (1896–1902) (Sevak Prakashan: 1980); Vol. V, *The Last Phase* (1946–48) (Navajivan Publishing House: 1966). Massive, unfinished biography by Gandhi's last secretary.